for Justus & Allegra, bright passages
& for Bill—who bravely "fathers forth"

BRIGHT EXIT

by Laurie Zimmerman

QUERCUS REVIEW PRESS

MODESTO, CA

2014

QUERCUS REVIEW PRESS POETRY SERIES
Sam Pierstorff, *Editor*

Published by Quercus Review Press
Department of English
Modesto Junior College
quercusreviewpress.com

Cover art by Carol Mortimore
Author photo by David Adams

Printed on acid-free paper
10 9 8 7 6 5 4 3 2 1

ISBN-13: 978-0692238530
ISBN-10: 0692238530

Publications by Quercus Review Press (QRP) are made possible with the support of the English Department at Modesto-Junior College. A portion of the proceeds from the sale of this book will benefit creative writing scholarships at Modesto Junior College.

CONTENTS

In the distance, dark before the bright exit,
stood someone whose face
could not be recognized.

—*Rilke*

OWL

The snow essential. Low
moan hung like a heard
moon across the flurrying
night. Light calling.
Body in its dress
of feathers and dust.
Hunched shape
shifting in the dark
fork of pine. Coo
and muffle, swivel-
fall flush. Bird
or snow or shadow.
Night's mean, equation
of fall-rise, song-silence.
Song as betrayal. Snow
as plenitude. Or
the other way around.

WHITE SHIP

She said she wanted to be brought back
to thinking the world could be good
in the natural sense, said, *I want physicality.*

Then sun laid the blue bruise of God's body
across her mountains just before evening   personification
tied the wind with black bandages.

Meantime she was sitting at the window
poking holes in the theory of sky
and all the stars singing their silences
by dropping notes out of range
of ears and the languages of the eye.

Though she cried, *Abba, Abba,*
she couldn't differentiate between longing
and the perfume of the nightbird's song.

She said, *If the weather were better,*
if the dog, if this friend hadn't died
horribly, if I could get on the good side
of the moon, but then she remembered
the astronauts who had been

to the darkness where she kept looking,
who penetrated the shadow with their white
ship and, in that way, ruined everything.

NIGHTWEATHER

The rain stops during the night
at the same time
you begin to feel the evening's slow angers

tire and dissolve.
Three a.m. and thirsty beyond belief,
beyond any ability to quench your sense

of personal injustices, sodden
with them. Suddenly the roof
thrumming above your bed

imagery

with commotion of a different dampness
gone silent and now
banging of the back gate

a neighbor has left open
as wind of a new front
barrels in and some litter or child's toy

in the parking lot next door
scrapes against pavement.
The hum of a refrigerator truck

at the minimart vibrates
like a quiet breathing next to you,
as when once

someone lay there sleeping
but as you moved
to touch his cool and lovely arm

he opened his eyes
to gaze at you—and you whispered
in drowsy breathiness,

the window exhaling the curtain,
air moving out and in
as if it were natural and would last.

BIRD

I'm happy this morning
to have learned the shape and colors
of a new bird, come to dip and eat

on my evergreen bushes, though I can't
find its name in the book, though I may never
learn the word for her, yet if I sit still

here in my window, observe
the oily tinge of the wings, tapered gray
end feathers crinkled like foil,

the mango down on the throat
I wish I could stroke, wouldn't she
come even closer to me?

My mother, the one I would ask,
who knows all the names of things—
who taught me to learn

the birds and the trees, flora and fauna
of America, is not here. Still, I'm glad
for the bird picking seeds on the pachysandra,

grateful that she grips one bobbing
slim branch with tiny noduled feet,
that she lifts her head with a seed.

Her beak against the gray stuns me—
sun-yellow. I love that when she swallows,
her neck and chest flutter—harden, then

soften, like a ripening time-lapse fruit.
For a minute, concentrating, she fixes
her me-side eye on the pane.

She doesn't know my name any more
than I know hers—vulnerable,
content in it, she watches me

with her small bright optic lens,
not a bead, pebble, black button,
nor reverse star, only an eye,

one creature approaching,
who sees or does not see,
through a window darkly, me.

SOMETIMES THE TREES

Sometimes the yellow leaves are just so . . .
and nothing, not even wind, can touch the
radiant quiet emanating from them.

Then someone, maybe this exuberant doublet of students
bursts in—green eyeliner, pink dreads, low jeans,
whirls round my desk with their brisk scowls, their kisses.

Liz leans on my shoulder, Cait squeezes onto my chair,
tells secrets I in my teachery love don't want to hear.
I'd bring them home if I could like perfect pears for my counter.

Sometimes the trees outside my room shed their leaves
one by one, as if autumn were a stylized routine.
Sometimes they strip their gold robes at once, as if trying   *personification*
to say, *We don't tease, this is it, everything.*

Sometimes the shed gowns of the trees are umber, ochre,
they're like old grocery bags kicked under cars. Sometimes
my favorite maples seem scornful, point their emptying arms
at my desk, hemmed these days by lemony, tube-lit fluorescence,

or maybe they laugh heartily at all my ideas about love.
Like a teacher, I stare back through the text of the window and ask,
What are you really saying? But they're too busy releasing their
        leaves,
not holding onto them, not even with the cold that's sure to come.

THROWING BACK

Voice on my machine, voice of my father
who calls every few years to say they haven't heard
from me. Voice of stumble and false buoyancy.
What can he want? What do I have
to tell him?

I woke feeling insubstantial, rising in the radon day
like steam from the heat duct, from the teacup,
and the phone ringing, ringing, upright
like a black fish pointed out of the sea, rattling
fish I can't grasp, can't throw
back into water.

Over the great hook of distance I turn
his voice over, take measure of the silver tail
at the end of a once-powerful strength,
all of it in my hands—slippery with
incrimination,

hands that don't know how to hold on
to that which wants to leap sunward.
Thing that once rose through granite, through reels
of graduated light, body of water, body of
graying stone, now soft enough
to swim through.

SKI JUMPER

My girl as air-
        borne, crimson-suited semaphore,
as four-pointed star,
        dark shadow-dot
of high swift over blank snow,
        far eaglet,
as glider plane held against a moment's
        obedience of sky.

My girl as earth, mountain blued by lupine,
        as high pine,
astringent wind over meadows
        alight with humming,
granite errata, druzy glitter of mica,
        crumbling, building,
as polished sand under lotic grasses,
        land without end.

My girl as fire,
        as bullet of my body,
searing tissue, velocity,
        the rocket's brilliant effacement,
my life without ripcord,
        blue flame of danger,
as torn organ of myself, tortuous circle,
        hemorrhage of desires.

My girl as water,
        as immersion,
the whole pond in stillness, gold pond in sun,
        beloved of enemies.
I tip back my head. I am a cup
        she keeps pouring, and
as she pours, I keep on,
        I fill up.

GOD SAID

1.

Let there be light
and there was,
and he nodded his cloudhead,

said, *Good.*
We take this
any way we wish,

literal, metaphoric,
the result's the same:
light, a good thing.

2.

Whenever my father told us
one of his stories,
someone was always being

ground up
in the blades of their
threshing machine

or eaten alive inch by inch
by a bear while camping
with a candy bar

or spit from the flatbed
of a truck on a road
with too many curves

because according to my father
the worst accidents
happen in the country

amidst the deceptions of beauty.
My father ended all his stories with
That's no joke! staring us down

with his cobalt eyes, his wild
Irish eyebrows. Today my sisters
and I, no longer appalled,

 will laugh and say,
when we break an egg,
That's no yolk!

My father was a tilt-a-whirl.
He tipped us upside down,
whipped us in furious circles,

kept us strapped
in the centrifugal fury
of our love and terror.

Now in middle age, I always
notice a little light inside
each spongy lung of egg.

3.
I have a friend who died
in that dumb-accident way
my father would love to tell

except for Tom, the accident
happened inside him, some gold beam
of himself split off, cell-burst

after cell-burst, a light in him gone
haywire. We know what the matter is,

never-ending, stars to dust to us

to dust of us, and we think
this is good, because in light of
everything, what else can we do?

Tom was the kind of guy
who'd hand me a drawing of a bathtub
he'd just sketched on a napkin

because I complained
I'd no one in my life
to draw me a bath.

4.

If time is a circle
the way some believe
then when God said

Let there be light, he meant
right now and also, in the past
which circles toward

a future. God could have
said, *There will be light,*
as in, there will always be this

holy spirit

bright in us, spinning
helix we don't see
though we are all the parts of it.

PURPLE FINCHES

Electric, isn't it, the little purple finches
come to nest in the ugly ornamental arborvitae

in front of my window, how they flicker, work
all day in brilliant heat bringing bits of timothy,

and all those gangly, grinning primroses beneath
taking over the garden I used to tend?

Last night, a constant slap of basketballs
on the courts, and too hot to cover my head

with my pillow, hug my body's loneliness with a sheet.
The dog fussed room to room sensing distant thunder

but it never came near us. She wouldn't lie down,
wouldn't go outside, I couldn't give her comfort.

You should learn to weed, get off the couch,
my mother said. I'd been sick for most of the year,

made my old mistake, called for sympathy.
Even the yellow faces of the primroses seemed shamed,

turned away as if it weren't the breezes turning them.
And those aren't purple finches, probably sparrows,

get a bird book, I've told you for years . . .
The whatever-creatures leave pieces of long grass

(probably not timothy) sticking horizontally
like sloppy chopsticks from the maybe-not-arborvitae.

That's why I'm sure they're still in love—
they fly to the eave, perch together looking at their home

through the staticky heat of afternoon, second by long second.
It's as if they cannot believe what they have done.

MAKING FALAFEL

Summer trees christmassed with winter white
lights shining toward ships in the working harbor below,

masts clanking. Ninety or so handblown
martini glasses from Mexico laid out on a plank,

Patrick pouring, wearing his pink sarong,
his grin. The other table overladen with food,

Stavros rearranging everything, even my own plate
so the appetizers look erotic, tiny sausages

cozied up to pairs of falafel.
Carol and I are laughing, dancing

around the patio in costumes—silver mermaid,
harem concubine, rhinestone heart sewn on my panties

pressed into the bone of my right hip, nearly invisible
under the fuchsia gauze of the pants. Then,

everyone else is dancing too—including the man
with the large night eyes, black curls

over his forehead and collar, gold skin on his bare arms,
black linen shirt, boots, black jeans, even in this heat.

Some guy teases he wants to wear my pants,
someone bending my ear with jokes, but I'm thinking

of something else—of the man with the sienna eyes
who has turned now, picked up the empty platter.

He's brought the falafel, maybe feeling responsible,
wants to replenish the dish, or wants to escape,

or isn't amused by the eroticism of his foodstuffs.
So he goes toward the house, but at the door

calls me as if maybe he needs me to help.
And we stand alone together in the candlelight

of the kitchen as he lowers, then swiftly lifts
each gilded egg of pressed bean from boiling liquid,

holds them up as they cool, jeweled with oil and dripping
like cakes kissed with honey. He places his warm hand

under mine on the spoon to show me how to raise it
without splattering. It all happens so fast, just like that.

Sensual

DINNER MUSIC

Over salmon and wine
the small birdmusic of a poem
keeps time in my ears

while I see the words
already flocking to the lines.

If it weren't so rude
I'd excuse myself for this
other language, leave the room,

give my hand its pen.
But we're together so rarely

over our glasses and you've taken
an olive into your mouth.
I notice the delicate precision

of your teeth as you separate
the briny meat from pit.

The corners of your lips
are wet when you place the stone
between your fingers,

hold it, then lean over into
my neck for a kiss.

The poem folds its wings
but another happiness
flies up.

AUBADE

Higher than you are
lower than both of us
astonishing month of winter.

You walk beneath
wan floors of sun. Dawn
is our home.

Deer leap back and forth
through white fields, eyes
spilling gold tea-light

antlering up like summer
swarms of bees
startled in the grass.

In morning you understand
yourself. More and more
you wild forward like the deer.

Is there something after
midlife love to think of?
Yesterday I remember

as night, the year before
as darker than night.
All the birds are finding the snow

hilarious, giddying it
with their beaks, hungry
and filled with pleasure.

Crows lower
the snowy branches, close
the hem of the light spaces between

till sky falls toward us. Up
from the field, covered in coming dark
leave slowly, only if you must.

TRANSPLANT

Gray vapor snugs up to the windows
from the granite pier below your house. You rise
to grind coffee, throw hummus and flatbread into
a pan, turn on CNN, bow your head at news from home.

The stone walls seep Rockport cold. Walking your beige
retriever, I'm wrapped like a mummy in flannel layers,
walk faster so I can get back to place her bowl in front of her.
She eats with the ecstasy of a trained dog in a commercial.

Evenings of wind and foghorns are my allies.
We bury ourselves in the white blanket your mother sent
from Egypt, drink wine, eat a happiness of figs and chocolate,
watch movies you copy illegally from the video store.

By summer, Cairo has exploded onto every screen. I feel uneasy,
you are disconsolate, begin to grow a sense of your disloyalty.
One day you feed me a few overcooked lines about how every-
thing, especially, I realize, you, is always moving on.

MOUNTAIN

Let's see the highest point of that mountain we climbed
as dual—angles of aspiration always eroding—

and we, mountain of what shouldn't have been but was
—bulk-store glassware, economical wine,

the front door locked against possibility, against
discovery. Let's admit the mountain

already crumbling the night we met, the surprise of it
and our eager hearts reluctant. Didn't Rumi say

*it's a bonfire at the top edge of a hill, this meeting again
with you?* When we kissed in the dark under an upended

moon, the sky was already moving away,
even the glacial scat your house squatted on

was migratory, even the sea-winds off the pier
were undressing the harbor of its sails.

love is fleeting

REFRAIN

I'm not waiting, I'm leaving
fast, going outside, leaving

with my one bag unzipped,
a piece of a blouse hanging

from the outer compartment,
leaving and knowing

there won't be goodbye,
clutch or slow tug

on my lips, my hips
pressed into your

hips. I'm heading out
under the sun's angry brilliance,

the sky green with leaf-glare.
I'm packing my car like a pistol,

I'm under the gun, the hot air's
aggravation of larch fronds.

I'm crushing my bare feet against
your new grass, hearing the

water's reports from the fountain
next door I'm already missing,

windows that watched us,
watching now, I'll miss, water,

leaves, grass, rock-trigger path.

I'm loaded and locked

into the barrel of my car, far from
the porch where you stand, arms folded

over your Kevlar heart,
guarding the house of your missing.

WHILE MAILING A LETTER

To want is to lose—everyone
knows this but I forgot.
The shriveled red berries
on the cherry tree are
unshielded from wind,
but the strongest fruit stays
aloft on ligneous wires
for two seasons, till beaked winter
comes with its creatures and cold sun.

Everything on a continuum
continuously ending—
summer, light, a book
I read for a month
slower and slower
so as not to reach the end,
and now even this stamp
I place on an envelope—
last one of the sheet
he bought for me
because I wanted
commemoratives:

extinct dune birds
amidst threatened grasses.
He'd held me in the wind
amidst erosions of sand.
He placed his warm hands
against my bitten cheeks
carefully and so long
I no longer knew my face
was still mine.

[handwritten annotation, left margin: "typical love poem"]

[handwritten annotation: "(wood)" pointing to "ligneous wires"]

32

THE FINAL YEAR

It was in that final year,
the dinner when you brought
week-old cake from your office
as your contribution, then drank
all the whiskey in the house,
leered at our host, molested me
in the hallway, slumped sullen
and drunk at midnight in a chair,
roared away in your car after
stealing the keys back from me.
That year I was always finding
my own ride home. Sometimes
you laughed loudly at dinner
when someone shared
a deeply held belief and always
I found you helping yourself
to other people's plates—I could
go on. The greatest thing
about the movies we watched,
twined like lumps of yarn on
your couch, was that time lost us
and you seemed to be entertaining
the idea of love. I couldn't help
it--I would give away my heart
just to feel your arm across
my hips, hear your nearly silent
breath as you slept. I don't remember
much else of that year but that
and how the harbor bells and foghorns
rose and died all night long,
moon sunk into the pine wind,
dawn scratching without
sound along the window screen.

,-LIES-BLEEDING

Six months ago, just before Good Friday,
       just before you would put on your robes and hold your
          hands up

over the homeless in your parish, the drug-addicted starving
          and the starving
          for love and you would pray for their souls with your
          eyes closed

       I wrote an email and blew up your job.

Nine months ago I wrote a letter to your wife,
       exploded any shred of respect she still had for you.

Twelve months ago you stopped calling, suddenly refused
       my name, my number, forgot you loved me, denied
       your promises,

       you were sleeping with someone else, forgot

to tell me. You ate through my heart as if it were a small cookie
       and you a voracious grenade, left it like a Jesus in the
         shape of an amaranth.

There's no putting someone back together after that--even the mind
       detonated, the limbs you used to hold numb as a tombstone.

       I took to shivering in a darkness for weeks,

didn't know where or what it was I was
       which was better than what followed, memory shot

but fumbling for a synapse among shrapnel, an invisible war
       raging in me--hate or hope and no telling the difference.

       That's why, more than a year after

you tore through the country of my life with your incendiary vices,
    I have no answer to the email you sent today,

asking for forgiveness, for friendship,
    a serpent twisted on a stick carved from poison and rubble

    what's left of either of our lives.

STILLNESS: MY REPLY

And when, in the city in which I love you,
even my most excellent song goes unanswered . . . .

~Li-Young Lee

Here in this village, where I'm learning
        to forget you,
the worst of all we've ever said
        replies to me.
I descend into the low meadow
        along the Blackwater,
cross the deer-tunneled hayfields,
        broad exposures of sun.

I'm lost here to a gentle clarity,
        light silent
as wet seeds
        muffled by earth.
I become a girl again, afloat on her back
        in the water,
        sculling through dazzles of current.
I drop my histories, move from you

through gold tassels, past crumbling tractors,
        the stony graffiti
of glaciers, birds in their churches of leaf
        along the licked paths of river,
its edges of chicory and pickerelweed,
        into the layered
quiet countryside where I am safe.

You are an old wound.   You lift off of me.
        Just as the body
eventually rises from its pallet of pain
        one way or another,
        I lose all memory
of you, your face shapeless, skin
        cool, unbeckoning,

every hour of your hard wingless grain
        a dome of ice, unreflective
        of me.

My lips forget your bruised scent, ache
        at the back of my mouth
when you kissed me, it rests.
        See how the light
        off the tops of my shoulders is gold,
        how the field shimmers
through each curl of my hair?

Rejected by rain, known only by finches now
        aloft over yellow walls of fieldstone,
my anonymity simplified by stillness,
        by forgiveness of myself,
in the quietude this close to silence,
        despite bird-hymn and bee-hum,
        if you listened
you could hear me closing my mouth.

AFTER THE MARRIAGE

Here I am in the yard
standing at the edge of the garden—
this used to be yarrow
tangling the stalks of black-eyed Susan
and the purple fizzed Joe-Pye weed,
and this, pink-cupped mallow,
over there a profusion of wild geranium
I would pull to relocate all summer.

Here I am before the shrubbery
of ragged forsythia, roots
crusted into a muck of fall leaves,
rake loose in my hand—
this used to be grass under my feet
and this, a marigold bed,
over there a yellow dog, two white chairs
turned toward the street.

BREATHING FROM MEMORY

You wake—birth or death—
 to white—what could be
filigrees of iced grass
in a valley of snow

or just this bed
of tangled wires
snaked across pale sheets.

Now you know
how soft some pain,
how it melds you
to the gentle plinth of the
pillow against your head,

your skull like
the cool skin of a plum,
wet curve
of a bottle of milk
back when good things
came right to your door.

What is it, what is it
when you merge with
a slow thought,
and you wish only
to watch the green-scrubbed
figures moving along a periphery
of the brilliant room?

One arm begins to feel
a pain something like
the compression of a perfect
key filling a lock,
then the small matter of
a turn,

springing a door
which unfolds outward,
which is to say, a wing,
its bright hinge
gathering air.

AFTER TEN HOURS

parts of me were gone, portions of my back,
chest, arm, chevron hole next to my heart
they left open to the bone . . . .

When I first woke from the anesthesia
I thought, I'm surrounded by a crowd—
people talking loudly, me watching and

wishing to keep looking from a distance
across the wide paddock, too soon become long
room, small table, finally curtained bed—

then I was alone, almost, holding Carol's hand,
the nurse carrying yellow, purple, red
flowers—jar a tall monument, reading the card

from ones I love, speaking my name
till I knew where I was. Today
the dried heap of deeply hued roses

in their high construction on the dresser
reminds me of a divided confounding,
the way you can walk down a hall

toward someone you may love,
yet not know for certain
whether he'll tender your name,

or tell you he forgets . . .
which is the same as a childhood
dream, that isn't a dream, that taught

one false move—tie your shoes sloppily,
forget to brush the bangs from your eyes,
put an unpleasant expression on your face—

a child could be orphaned for days.
I loved the red petals' extroversions, the purples'
purgations, the yellows' scorched retractions at the edges,

then my name sprawled largely across the card,
With Love, and after, the words of my friends,
which Carol announced for the nurses,

how the interns crowded around
the preposterous blossoms,
my errant-outrageous bouquet—

scooped burn-gold blooms nodding down
from their tower, velvet jesters painted
like wounds, my arrangement of beautiful fools.

VISITING HOURS

I am strapped into the crumpled bed
of my body—can't rise, can't
uncrease myself, so when you
come to see me with your
wool scarf tied tightly
throughout your visit, like the
visible garrote of your witness guilt
I can't help but think, This is one more thing.

I release you by saying
I'm tired—not tired truly, though
the bones in my chest wall ache
but so that we can both believe
in a world of generosity
when you take your leave of me.

IN PROCTOR GRAVEYARD
for Don

During illness, it's mostly women who stay near,
except for the few, remnant I remember, I celebrate,
who fly cross-continent to make me eat, leave
endearments on my machine, tell me the jokes
that keep me alive, and especially the one

who drives me to chemo though it costs him
the memories of his own terrible history,
but these men I count on less than a hand.
It's the Marys who come fluttering

like acres of scarves, all busyness and tears,
arms filled with casseroles, paintbrushes,
cookies, their lists, and treats for the dog.
They don't shrink from my scars, they touch me

as if I'm still human but try not to hug me
too hard. Their eyes follow me crossing the room.
Sometimes I believe they're viewing
a documentary of their futures so I try not to die.

After autumn, when snow covers the windfalls
under the trees and the pretty graveyard empties
of visitors, I walk alone in my close cap, so thin
and pale I could lie down next to Jane, not get up.

I hold Gus's collar to my lips, don't feel the buckle's
cold kiss. Snow keeps falling, a few maple leaves
laying hands on Donald's name. My mouth wants
to scrape his ten letters clean of them with the metal
blade the chemists have pressed into my tongue.

THE COUNTRY OF LEFT AND RIGHT

Later they offer to tattoo my new nipple with vermilion.
I say, *Yes, please*, sweet for a change—after all,

what're a few needles of pink when I've had so much blue
electric juice injected every which way through my veins—

more chemistry than the fevers in the brain I've fought all my life?
This morning surgeons with clean perfect hands and sympathy-smiles

plan the mound of breast to cover the pound of flesh God's exacted
from me—smacking me upside the chest for my sins,

times innumerable I looked askance at him. I began
disbelieving after years of my failures to please, now lie

wired on a tubular bed ticking like a Geiger counter, register
of every wrong in the world. Somewhere TV news keeps blaring,

here my tears fall past my ears onto the gurney.
I'm smart/stupid, rich/not—no matter—they slap me back together.

Today they thread metal through my good breast, tomorrow
tunnel muscle from my back to replace the bad. In my nation, the good

breast is an affluent country—has manageable malignancies it shares
with the world secretly, calls that charity, perhaps is my ally for years.

CELEBRATION FRAGMENTS

1.

The TV announcer calls the celebrity
with breast cancer *heroic* for surviving.
She gives money to my oncology ward.
Another channel tells me my stomach
will flatten if I buy an ab-spatula machine.

It's spring and that means Easter,
more light—something to celebrate.
I throw out the houseplants
I've killed off during winter.

The papers say the troops make headway
though civilians stick to dying.
CNN, children's bodies, photos:
no one's got a leg to stand on.

The church in East Andover has put up
their sign. It's official: Jesus Is Risen,
three exclamation points. He must be
the lucky one this spring. And still

I keep thinking, hope never hurts
enough—it comes when all is lost
and comes again, like a relentless
lover, calling. . . .

Oh, Jesus, Christ of Attachment,
I am hooked on everyone. Christ!!!
of the pond and almost bursting pods
of seed, I love all
the freshest wetness of the new.

2.

When I was sick for a year,
ice like glass cocoons

around the pine needles glittered—
in sun or cloud-cast or
with the heavy bag of moon.

Steel needles dripped their cold
shards through my arm while winter
shimmered like a celebrity's long neck.
Only the chewed veins remain, some scars

inside my elbow.   So today I feel lifted
like the small tumors of buds rising on
the limbs of my ornamental cherry trees.
And those memories, already fading—a night

I heard the neighboring mini-mart broken
into—in my suffering the only one awake,
smashing of the front door
a metallic cough, so like the sound

of the radiation room sealing shut
behind me. I clutched my chest,
couldn't reach out
to call the cops.

3.

For years my children
inhabited emergency rooms, their father
couldn't find their jackets, his keys,
wallet, glasses, later his own
health. I believe I have held steady.

I wanted to marry a man
who could walk on water or the moon,
but now I'll marry only me.
I'll vow to keep myself forever. I think
of my life as a lifting through heavy liquid—

that fluid blackness, like when the bulb
of amaryllis you placed there breaks
and thrusts a long arm upward—
despite the bed of stones,
the bowl of dark you forced it in.

REMISSION

You can't make sense of anything.
If you say fine, you're lying.

On the best days you almost forget
you'll always be this patient.
Your happiness is brief, hard as a table.

Every bird, each slant of light
has been bought by blood and vomit.

On ordinary days, your arm
is useless, lymphy. It pulls at
the adhesive fires in your shoulder.

Your fingers engorge. They can't hold
anything. If someone were to
love you now how would you know?

On bad days, you think of
parts of things you might be like . . .

shrunken bole on an apple branch,
cold shoulder of broken windfall fruit.

On good days, other people's pleasures
grate. Even the dog rolling
on the rug is a circle of sorrows.

On bad days, everything, reddish finches,
indigo jays, is a catastrophe in color. There's
no soft field to fall in.

The phone keeps ringing, keeps ringing.
Someone is saying goodbye. Someone
is saying I'm dying and hello.

TOUCH

At the pond, small moon
appearing over the silent body,
tender water beginning

to show caplets, the
webs laddering through pines.

I in midnight blue bikini
and low light—scars glowing
like sorrowful leeches)

as I swim, then stand dripping,
examine with my hands a new thing

I call my self but don't see
yet as me, which is why
I slink off in darkness to swim—

sliced back, slug-cross
of armpit, breast I can't feel

or recognize . . . yet how
the world's body writhes
in more dire heat, I tell myself,

my scars less
than a jar of caught fire.

Yet every wound has its own mind,
its own body. Some days they
grow fists, wad tickertapes of pain,

pound their pink histories
into each pulsebeat, other days close

like earth's arteries, but ooze the slow
magma of sadness—wounds decide
when to pluck every nerve, when to die,

Now the loons have gone
to their nests, no doves call,

no skunks shuffle in the underbrush.
A bat comes for mosquitoes, then another,
scoring the pond with their scissordips

where I stand, and here I am
in wet kisses, a cool silver touch.

THE WEIGHT OF WINGS

The sun drops its one black shoe on the mountain,
evening kneels down in gray skirts. The cicadas
stop throbbing from the ring of wild cherry, branches
hung with moons of silk sacs. *Everything retreats,*
surges, circles, but doesn't end, you told me. I stand
at a graveside, two friends, where the bushes we planted
have rambled, have gone completely mad. Each life
has its own idea of heft—I think of the mussels' blue doors,

thin wings opening and closing on tiny hinges;
they withstand the tides that knock a boat over
or pull a grown man under. I asked you, *What is it*
when love pins your heart like a butterfly clipped to a board?
You said, *What is it when you wish to be kept there,*
weighted under the glass though it kill you?

REDUX

Too late the autumn mothwings
coming apart in my cupped hands,
dusting my pants as I race to the door
to let her fly off, prevent
her immolation in my candles.

But then the kids scuffle into the picture
of my domestic dishevelment,
unraked leaves, mower uncovered,
beach toys that never made it to the garage

and though the dog died months ago
did I not have a heart small or hard enough
to harvest the neon crop
of her tennis balls from the lawn?

My students toss one to me now
but I have the moth to hold
and they tease, *Hey, graded our papers?*
We're headed for Boston, wanna come?

All the trees judder with wind,
limbs stoned on autumn—I don't think
I've felt this in years—I tell the kids that
and they laugh, get in their car

just as I notice the moon over them
has this Wyf of Bathe tonnage of scarves
around it, and I wonder why
I'm terrified of any word like *pilgrimage*—
why a friend can say *journey*

and someone needs to bring me the salts.
The sky's darkened early and the trees,
though locomotive, are taking no passengers
under the heavy wool moon,

then there's me, alone in the drive,
wanting my life to be like the kids' car
turning around now on my road,
headphoned heads draped out the windows,
all of them shouting, *Are you sure?*

HAPPINESS INTERRUPTED BY BLESSING

If someone gave out choices
then maybe this morning—
leaves thick around the windows—

how they almost erase the memory
of snow . . . and an hour
just passed, when happiness

in a form close to not thinking
of you approached,
interrupted by coming across your note.

Why hadn't I thrown it away?—
cryptic handwriting, red pen,
your *just to say* difficult as an old poem.

I know—I'm ridiculous; I'm hyperbole—
and anyway, if God gave us choices
on a morning of leaves and windows—

no cold to speak of for months—
I remember, you love heat as I do—
I'd probably still choose this last hour

bereft as I am of you
if one is ever bereaved
of someone she never had

and if God's even there
as you seem to believe,
saying to me when I tell you

I love you most in the world,
God bless you,
I who possess only the shard

of a soul left, finding no solution
having thrown the rest of it
windward, though perhaps

still hoping the grackles of God
might flash the sheen of their wings
once more for me—spittle

of their master's final meal—
and gather that one piece—souvenir?—
I don't know, maybe something

to press in the lintel of a pearl gate
or to place under the heel of a saint
but that's me, thinking evil . . . gnash of teeth.

If I had a soul like yours, not made
shard, not caught like phlegm
in the throat of a bad god

I could love purely . . .
if my heart had been held
in your hands . . . but that was impossible.

When we stopped talking by phone
and I fell, not toward your voice
but your arms, my heart was

clear liquid, it ran through your fingers,
you never even saw it.
I mean to say, how can people love

when they're water?
How can people touch
when to do so is to dissolve?

AFTER OUR DIAGNOSES

Walking through white birches, yellow afternoon,
October—month of your birth—
my hurt, your voice echoing from that last time
we argued, I lean into the split
between amazement and disease—this deepening
into beauty and our griefs
as when slung over the side of a rocking boat once
after a late swim

I felt terrified, torn by the sight of the moonlit phosphors
mingling with my bio-lumined vomit—
then for a moment could not negotiate
the loveliness I saw
before my eyes and the wretchedness I felt
would be my life.

THING WITH FEATHERS

Last night, elation—I mention because of the dark,
waning moon and how rare—awake, pacing,

to know your difficulty but feel this

strange change-up of joy. You had called, yes,
your voice a thing I imagine an addict feels

when the sweet junk is sent directly to the vein,
but it wasn't that. Earlier I'd slept

in the sun, dreamt weirdly I'd sent you
a carrier bird you hadn't returned

and you so ill, declining. . . .

I woke drowsy, burned, half-crying, for a moment
wondered if you'd died, convinced my dream

was the message. Later, meditating, bowed on the rug,
I heard scratching—the window—raised my eyes.

This is no lie—a gray dove hovered, trying
to walk up the pane, flurry of feathers, wings

—you'll think I'm insane—it looked at me, kept looking,

seemed to hang on the glass an infinity
before it arched back,

back and back—before it swooped free,
then flew fast

toward the airy and radiant trees.

AFTERWORD
April 2008, in memory of Jason

1.

The puddled sidewalk. Abandoned scaffoldings.
I thought the rain in cold sheets a perfection.
Trees trying to leaf. That wet green. Then sudden sun.
As if to say what I could not feel.
We go on. Even without.
Which seems anathema.

2.

Dear ones,
we are animal. Sometimes
it's hard to know this. Especially today.
But there is also the way,
there and not there,
he was a wall,
impenetrable, protective, often invisible
the way a good wall is.
Night seawall.

3.

There are happy couples, a bright café.
Cars glide by shining.
I've driven six hours in a torrent
to know. What cannot be.
The carnage of streets turning beautiful,
so many trees blooming.
I wander. It's over.
Walking under blossoms like an opossum,
head down, sniffing the intoxicant of decay.

THE WAY THE DARK DOES

Thank you for staying
long enough
to say I love you
just one month
before dying so
your last words
never had time
to be ruined by
missing calls and
rumors and gaps
between emails
that said you'd forgotten
or refused or felt
mystified or agitation
found you or
misgivings or
awkwardness or
anger or
worse, indifference
but none of that
could happen anymore
once you died so
it was a clean
end, your arm over
my shoulder as if
to say yes, finally
it's over and I love you
can stay.
When I heard
you died I
pulled to the shoulder
of the road
and sobbed
till a cop appeared
illuminating the inside

of my car
flashlight strobing
back and forth
catching my face
the way the dark does
till I could no longer
see anything
but the fresh-
terrible bright
around me.

IN THE VILLAGE OF SNOW

Before the day drops its tonnage of gray,
all night the pelting of false light—
beams of the plows sweeping the windows

along my east wall, thrashing the empty side
of the bed. Also the wind, swan-necking
one birch onto the shutters. People say,

At least you're alive, which makes sense
if living were this

kicking into the swift river of cold—closed
storefronts, cloaked doorways, hunched yards.

I wonder which atoms of white air might be you,
now that you're apart, part of all the light we know.
Perhaps you've built another village of yourself

elsewhere, no longer present here,
even in these ashen molecules I keep breathing—

not in the bowl I raise to my lips, not in your book,
worn pages like a torn fan, not in the ripples of ice
on the sill, nor the tiny holes mice have punched

in the drifts, nor in the spaces between
leafless branches that offer their bones to the trees.

The relentless plows drop their shovels onto the pavement,
scrape the spaces called *road*—which is its own kind of emptiness.
All the cars have gone home, but where is your home,

you who've become an invisible stitch between
a past and what's to come—out of my whole life's span
only a glance of quick light, ping of a star spiraling,

already gone the moment one admires it, or like my hand
on the windowful of dusk, which leaves no imprint of heat
but comes away wet? In this village of snow, dangling lines.

I write into wind, into dark: if you can't be with me,
be a candle, instead of a village empty of stars.

READING ON AN IONIAN BEACH

When I thought I wanted a faraway place
I meant these white stones along turquoise water,

I meant water I can swim in all day
and not meet another person,

water so calm that even I who's easily frightened
paddles around like a child freely

cove to cove with my awkward sidestroke
because in the ocean my injured arm

is buoyed—I'm finally limber—
and when I said I needed this trip

I meant the way the color of water here
somewhere between the hue

of my boy's leaf-colored eyes and the blue
of my own seeps into the portals of the body

and is translated by the mind
as happiness—yes—so that when I opened

my magazine today in this place
and happened to read about my friend's death

even though when I knew I had to get away
I also meant from my grief

I found it hard to breathe for a moment,
then caught myself smiling at the sea

that he loved so much and I thought how funny
he, jokester, would find the scene—

my escape to a faraway country first time
in my life but with his still finding me

and he now in his own faraway place
but glossed and famous over here.

HUSBAND

After you picked fruit all morning
in the orchards of your new family
you walked under the wet poplars

into town, opened your book
at a small podium on a worn brown desk
and began to teach
conversational English.

I'm angry you had to
walk miles in that cold rain

angry you stood on your feet
for eight hours of classes

then walked home again
in the freezing dark
to drink potato broth.

My memories of you are old:
a head full of dense curls, lean body
hunched over your guitar or
crouched behind homeplate.

For many years you've been ill
and for many years you haven't been
my husband.

When light rises each day
on my side of the ocean
and touches your empty side
of the bed, I open my eyes and think

you've already lived
more than half my day to come.

It's a comfort
this way you've always had
of walking ahead of me. I get up

to step through each minute, move
across the gold floorboards, this minute

dress, this minute wash my face, this minute
drink the coffee you sent for Christmas, this minute
stand before the peeling window

see how the vapors lift almost invisibly
from the patchy ground
you used to seed for us each spring.

USELESS SUGAR

After the noon nonshadows of roadside dogs
        a brief swale

under old-growth oaks' innumerable insects
        their o-magnificats
                vibrating
                in breezeless sun

and my no-longer-loves-me
        beside a universe of chorus
                mine a dirge mine a crushed plinth
                on which the finches won't alight.

It has to take more mettle
        a flock of steel-winged forks
        to wrench a body from stuporous grief

extract a wrecked heart from the accident
        of me.

I've come up from the meadow's
        sticky river
                dwindling along its banks

and out on the road the paper decks of ice cream
        grow soggy in the back of the ringing truck
                but no one there to buy

useless sugars and no sense I say
        in counting wingbeats
        only you hear coming.

The geese are restless—try
        unravelling the sky.

Sometimes if we're very good at love
what we give spills over
the little dam of ourselves

and now we're water
trickling in a volume only dogs can hear.

For years to be afraid of rivers
was to know in some insect way a secret

scratching at the grasses of my unconscious
how far from me one droplet
carrying the atoms of everyone I knew
can flow.

Now in the abandoned neighborhood of myself
unmistakable fugues

underground larval pools, sweet trees'
cicada songs tolling
winter come sudden, come still.

POETRY CLASS

I ask for an inspiring thought
and a student volunteers. *Paris Hilton*
believes every woman should own

three animals: a mink to wear, a jaguar
to drive, and a jackass to sleep with.
The class laughs and I give what I hope

is the kind of stare that says,
You are an idiot. *Sometimes*
I can see the wisdom in infanticide

is what I really want to say,
but instead I read a poem about the body
in which the physical self is the speaker

who talks graphically about
the physics of sex—a series of soft and hard,
pulleys, levers being the general idea—

and the students start to take
an interest again in the possibilities
for a poem to say something pertinent

to the steamed up factory floor
of themselves. I'm a panderer,
is what I'm thinking, poems on the dole

like pardons, for people who only want
to finger the bones. Some days, I feel like
a crippled car, side of the road, snow

and no bandanna for the antenna. Paris
has it right—I need a mink to keep me warm,
jag with heated seats, jack to lift me

out of the night's cold ditches.
They're supposed to be writing but someone's
humming the theme song to "Jeopardy,"

someone's resetting their watch and it beeps
like a tiny UPS truck backing up along their arm.
Last night the neighbors' little dog, a terrier I think,

barked for hours before succumbing to exhaustion—
then only a whimper every five minutes.
If you'd told me at three in the morning

this would be the rest of my life, I would have
believed you, I would have run next door
in my flip flops and pajamas and strangled that dog,

then used the leash on myself. But today
humidity is draping the trees, the world
cozying up to itself, and I feel more humble than usual,

more snug than smug. I feel swathed
in dampness and warmth, so when the students
bow their heads and pray to the poems begun

on their desks, my life begins speaking for itself
in the form of a question, and I know someone's
getting ready to write the correct answer.

PSYCHIATRISTS

Someone asks, How many psychiatrists does it take to change
      a light bulb,
     but my question is, why would anyone want to know?
I mean, aren't we all pretty much in the dark anyway,
     else why would we need a shrink,
let alone more than one, and if we go to one, or more than one—
     example: my friend who sees one for individual therapy,
one for group, then couples, another just for meds.,
     plus the one she goes to for fun
(she can't bear to tell him she's seeing all the others,
     won't hurt his feelings, she started his career, after all),
and there's the substance counselor too, because God knows, if
      you were
     paying for all that therapy, you'd take drugs too—
so, if we go to a psychiatrist, best to be in the dark,
     lie down, close our eyes, not see the bored look on his face,
the yawn when we moan for the hundredth time we're in love—
     wildly, hopelessly, inappropriately, with the one man
we know who's suicidally unavailable—maybe gay—though
     he hasn't figured that out yet, preferring to lure women in
with the flirtatious worm of his uncertainty, then dangle them over
     the smoldering waters of their own need till their mouths
      bleed.
Nicer if the room with its awkward piles of notes,
     stacks of textbooks, wavery blue-tube glow of computer
were left out of the picture altogether.   Preferable not to open
     our eyes or, if we must, better not to change the bulb.

NEW MOON

I know you're suffering, she tells me. *Hey, it's hot here*
in Texas. The roses are spazzing all over the yard,

I tell her the moon's a mean hook and all the stars swing
off it, guttering, my heart's the sky replete now with dark—

let's buy new sheets for our sons—what mother wouldn't?
a big ruthless mouth, full of sharp instruments, open for business,

I'd send you a card, but that's not enough—pretend it's a CAR.
the moon's snaggle-tooth catching the ruined lip of my night.

Honey, you don't need him, you're depressed.
You need a man, not a pencil-neck, not a stick insect.

When the moon's not around, my northern meadows lie down,
the fields raise their vapors above the river unconfounded,

You need yoga, a support group, you need your needs met,
you need mojitos, you need to be shaken not stirred,

and the waters keep rising, as the mist over them rises,
as the fog in my low valley rises, and no one thing stands out—

you need someone who loves the reality-flower of your body,
someone intimate with psychiatry not psychosis—

not a sentinel tree, not a ghost outline of deer, mound of feathers,
bit of dropped blossom, broken shell, piece of scree.

THIS IS THE YEAR

I forego the furniture, walk far
from the brown leather chair,

let go the couch you couldn't
rest on without ruffling my hair,

also the stove always simmering
with your tilapia and sauces,

let the air clear of your
lavenders from Egypt,

let go the falsities of nonfiction,
love sonnets and mysteries,

cling to parables, prodigal that I am,
woman porcine with demons,

beggar wind-scuttled like a shirt
blown across open road.

I forego the lamb baffled
and broken on the cliff,

as well as the shepherd, bent over
the burden between rock and wolf.

Gone is the hooked limb of olive
held out, empty of fruit. I am

the lone ewe bleating, the sheepdog
howling at an indifference of moon.

This is the year I forego
the empty field of that moon.

LIVING ALONE

I brushed my teeth while weeping
over the missing child
whose mother cried on a.m. news.

I walked down my road
to work, under leaves
small and brown as kittens

pattering in a litter of limbs—
smiled back at the man I know
behind his carmine tractor's wheel.

Then I didn't think once of
the sharp angles of children's bones
in photos of somewhere else.

When I was young I knew
how to swing so high
I could kick the pigeons

off the roofline of the school.
I spent all day behind bricks
hearing my teachers speak

and I never mentioned
what I'd seen—the head pulls
a body forward, the shoulders

bear the head, make a downward
bow around the body's cavity.
When I walked home today

it was as if a blue comb
had raked the tangles
from the skeletal trees

and on the silent phone
I carried, I saw the moon
was calling, and no one

but the umber husband of
my doorway to know
what I was missing.

ON CATCHING MYSELF 35 YEARS LATER
IN A STORE WINDOW

I think
        that woman may as well be dead.

I think
        all women of a certain age are beautiful.

I see my mother walking toward me.
I see the same plumpy black coat my grandmother always wore.

I remember
        looks are an illusion
        as are mirrors, commercials, Elizabeth Taylor's
        eyes called lavender.

And candlelight—especially candlelight, the necessity
        for a dark table.

I think
        when the Emperor wore no clothes, it was about
        an Emperor and not about my belief I'm 21.

I think
        the hair blowing across her face
        can't be that straight, that beige
        instead of the cascade of red curls I know it is.

On the pop news, what's trending. New rule: girls
        wear miniskirts again but never women over 45.
That begs the question
        what about bathing suits, sex
        with the lights on,
        training for the Ironman, pelvic exams?

Truth is
        a woman in a window is either a mannequin or a whore.

Who giveth this passerby to be wed to so few possibilities?

I see her
       slump her shoulders forward
       the same way I always do.

I see a girl
       looking awkward in her shoes
       the way she used to on the playground,
       kneesocks swimming downward, nipping at her heels.

HOW TO SWIM

through red leaves
  a dark cedar rinse
early autumn, after illness
  body of tender, difficult water
tangle of lilies, release of
  white cups, and
now they drift past me
  bluebottles, green dragon-
flies mottling the shallows.
  My dominant arm useless
my other must pull me
  to the center, around
the bend of the pond's elbow
  and what
of the ledges of the mountain
  overhanging, precipitous
their shadows?—out here
  no dock, no kayaks—alone
except for occasional moose
  tiny on the shore
or a loon that glides toward me—
  so close!
then changes direction
  ducking under, gone.
In deep water, out of reach
  of the insect-heavy trees
nothing but to lie back—small dented
  boat tilting in sun.
This far out, this deep in
  how the pond must become
all the parts the body is
  bereft of
even the mind, even the sky
  crossing itself
with kettling hawks
  falling up.

BRIGHT EXIT

Wilding of ferns, water's edge
      stillness
               spiral and spore
or his voice returned to the earth.

Under the water
             ruthless as loss
      incalculable stones.

One year since we died.
      A murder of words
            tapping alphabets
across longings of field.

On the feeder goldfinches, doves
      but I've preferred a dappling
            grackles, sparrows
graying the lawns.

A peckish ache residing
      at the back of my eyes
         reminder
I've looked too long at night signs while driving.

The tasks of the survivor
      carrying out the trash, restoring
        a handle to a drawer
           filling the mower with gas

I hoped to speak for me. There's a feeling
      a sureness of slide
        your foot slipping into a sandal
your hand reaching a rock waterside

your grief taken up, palmed and warm
      changed from harm

to this necessary
held arrangement of form.

ACKNOWLEDGEMENTS

Much thanks to the following publications in which some of these poems have appeared, sometimes in slightly different versions:

5 AM, "Happiness Interrupted by Blessing"; *Andover Beacon*, "Husband," "Ski Jumper"; *Crab Orchard Review*, "Sometimes the Trees," "Thing with Feathers"; *New Letters*, "After the Marriage," "Bird," "In Proctor Grave-yard," "Ski Jumper"; *Oberon,* "Stillness: My Reply"; *Poet Lore*, "Refrain"; *Rattle*, "Purple Finches"; *River Styx*, "Psychiatrists"; *Verse Daily*, rpt., "After the Marriage."

"Husband" received the 2014 Center for the Arts Poetry Award. "After the Marriage," "Bird," "In Proctor Graveyard," and "Ski Jumper" received the 2008 *New Letters* Award in Poetry. "The Country of Left and Right" received Honorable Mention in the 2008 *River Styx* International Poetry Contest. "Psychiatrists" won the 2008 *River Styx* International Poetry Contest. Five poems from *Bright Exit* were nominated for the 2008 Pushcart Prize.

In addition, my deepest gratitude to:

Ethney McMahon, Susan Norris, and Sarah Will—for extraordinary critiquing skills, support, and love.

Carol Mortimore—for the cover art and lifelong sisterhood.

Paula Closson Buck, Elizabeth Claman, and Clifton Ross—for manuscript scrutiny and abiding friendship.

Tony Hoagland, Ed Ochester, and Jason Shinder—beloved mentors.

Donald Hall and Michael Waters—for writing support and life support, beyond all reasonable expectations of camaraderie.

The doctors, nurses, and staff of Dartmouth-Hitchcock Medical Center and the Norris Cotton Cancer Center, including Charlene Gates, Da-Shih Hu, M.D., and Gary Schwartz, M.D. Also, Susette Milnor; and Marga Massey, M.D., and staff—for miracles.

Finally, to Liam Rector, the Bennington Writing Seminars, Proctor Academy, and writing communities in Squaw Valley, New York State, Montpelier, and Lithuania that helped me write this book—my humble thanks.

ABOUT THE AUTHOR

LAURIE ZIMMERMAN's work has been featured in *New Letters, Poet Lore, Paterson Literary Review, River Styx, Crab Orchard Review, Orion Magazine, Rattle, 5 AM, Oberon, Christian Century, Mid-American Review, Image,* and elsewhere, and online at *Verse Daily* and the Academy of American Poets website, among others. Zimmerman is the recipient of the *New Letters* Award in Poetry and the *River Styx* International Poetry Contest prize. *Bright Exit*, her first full-length collection, was a finalist for the May Swenson Poetry Award, the Agnes Lynch Starrett Poetry Prize, and the Washington Prize, among others. Her poetry has been featured on New Hampshire Public Radio and she was the recipient of a writing fellowship from the Univ. of New Orleans. A chapbook of her poems, *Hidden Branches,* was published in 1984. She is former poetry editor at *Radix* Magazine, Berkeley, CA, and she has taught English for 25 years at Proctor Academy, Andover, NH.

CPSIA information can be obtained at www.ICGtesting.com
Printed in the USA
LVOW10s1225110115

422375LV00002BA/280/P